Also by Susan Barnett Braun:

I Love to Tell the Story: Growing Up Blessed and Baptist in Small Town Indiana

For Young Adults:

Not So Happily Ever After: The Tale of King Ludwig II

For Children:

Sophie, Pay Attention (Rhoda, You Too)!

A Dog Called Naaman

Kate Middleton, Duchess of Cambridge:
A Biography for Children

Susan Barnett Braun

Photographs courtesy of Wikimedia Commons

Cover, Tom Soper Photography

Chapter 2, Pam Brophy

Chapter 5, Peter Gordon

ISBN: 1484130774
ISBN-13: 978-1484130773

Prince William and Kate leave Westminster Abbey after their wedding

April 29, 2011

CONTENTS

Prologue

Catherine Middleton, known to most of the world as Kate, glanced around at the thousands of eyes staring at her. She was a bride and this was her wedding day. Slowly, she walked down the aisle at Westminster Abbey, holding tightly to her father's hand. Beautiful music echoed around her, and she tried to remember each moment as the sunlight shone down on her through the stained glass windows.

There was her mother, on the left. And to the right, Queen Elizabeth gazed at her with a slight smile. Straight ahead was her groom, Prince William. Each dream-like step brought her closer to him. As she reached her prince, he smiled and whispered, "You look beautiful!"

Catherine took a deep breath. This was the day she had dreamed of, but it had taken many years to arrive here.

Prince Charles, Princess Diana, and President & Mrs. Reagan

Chapter 1

A Prince is Born

June 21, 1982: In London, the longest day of the year was coming to an end. Thundering cannons and cathedral bells broke into the warm, still night. Outside Buckingham Palace, a town crier announced that a son had been born to Charles and Diana, the Prince and Princess of Wales.

The baby's name was William, and someday he would become king.

Thirty miles away in Berkshire, Carole Middleton sat watching the television news about Prince William. She held her five-month-old baby, Catherine, on her lap. How exciting that her daughter and the new prince were so close in age!

Carole had been a flight attendant for several years, and this is when she met Michael Middleton, who ran operations on the ground at the airport. They married in 1980, and Carole decided to quit her job and stay at home when their first child, Catherine Elizabeth, was born on January 9, 1982.

Two years later, another daughter, named Philippa, was born. The family called her Pippa, and from the beginning she was more outgoing than the often-shy Catherine.

The Middleton family was complete in 1987 when son James arrived. Even though Carole was busy with her three children, she sometimes became bored. She began to wonder what type of job she could do that would still allow her to spend time with her children.

One day, Carole sat at the kitchen table, making up treat bags to send home with children who came to parties at her house. She sighed. She had made up so many of these bags over the years!

Mrs. Middleton had an idea. Why not start a business where she could make up wonderful treat bags for children and sell them to other mothers? This seemed like a great idea, and so she began a company called Party Pieces.

At the time, the Middleton family had no idea how successful Party Pieces would become. But within two years, Carole was selling so many treat bags that Michael was able to quit his job and work with the family business. Party Pieces started a website, and they began selling all kinds of party decorations, not just treat bags. They filled a barn behind their house with balloons, toys, games, and other trinkets, and the children helped their parents gather the items to fulfill orders. Catherine and Pippa even modeled dress-up clothes for the company's catalog!

Carole wanted to inspire other mothers to create magical

parties and to make party organizing a little easier, and she loved doing that through Party Pieces. She had always enjoyed entertaining, and she delighted her children with special birthday cakes. Years later, Catherine especially remembered "an amazing white rabbit marshmallow cake Mummy made when I was seven!"

When she wasn't helping with Party Pieces, little Catherine enjoyed dressing up like a clown and playing a game called musical statues. She liked to visit England's beautiful Lake District with her family on vacations. But soon she would leave her cozy family home for school.

Entrance to St Andrew's School

Chapter 2

Catherine Goes to School

Catherine went to St. Andrew's School, four miles from her home. Strangely enough, the university she later attended had the same name.

St. Andrew's was an expensive school that Mrs. Middleton called "the kind of school I dreamt of going to but could never afford." Thanks to the success of Party Pieces, the Middletons could afford to send their children there.

Catherine loved St. Andrew's. She was quiet, but loved to participate in sports. She joined the volleyball, basketball, tennis, swimming, hockey, and track teams. During her final year at St. Andrew's, when she was 13, she was named best all-around sportswoman for the school.

One of her most thrilling moments at St. Andrew's happened when Prince William visited in 1992 with his school team to play in a hockey match. There was huge excitement as St. Andrew's students tried to catch a glimpse of the royal prince, and 10-year-old Catherine was no different. Just imagine that twenty years later she and Prince William would get married!

Catherine filled her time with more than just sports. She also danced in The Nutcracker ballet and acted in several school plays. In one play, she played the part of a girl who falls in love with the wealthy man of her dreams. The man's name was William!

When she was 13, Catherine finished at St. Andrew's and enrolled in a new school. It was called Downe House, and it was quite different from St. Andrew's. Downe House was an all-girls school, and many of the girls lived at the school. Catherine still lived at home and only attended during the days. She soon learned that Downe House was not the wonderful place that St. Andrew's had been.

Buildings at Marlborough College

Chapter 3

Bullies and New Beginnings

At Downe House, Catherine learned some hard life lessons. Several girls bullied her. Why? There were no big reasons. Some said it was because she was shy. Others said it was because she was "not pushy enough."

Whatever the reason, Catherine spent a miserable few months at the school. She was shoved and tripped in the halls. Instead of being cheered on the playing field, she was kicked. Her school books and supplies disappeared mysteriously. Catherine was homesick and found it hard to make friends with the other girls who lived at the school and didn't want to welcome someone new into their group.

At Christmas, Catherine begged her parents to let her change to another school. When they learned how bad things had gotten, they agreed. In April, Catherine switched to Marlborough College.

Although it's called a college, Marlborough is not a college in the American sense. It is a boarding school for students aged 13-18. Both boys and girls attended Marlborough, and even though Catherine needed to leave her home to live there, she was much happier at Marlborough than she had been at Downe House.

Catherine's happiness had not come cheaply for the Middletons. A year at Marlborough cost $35,000, but Party Pieces was doing so well that they could afford the best for their children. By this time, the company had 30 employees and the Middletons had moved to their dream home, which they named Oak Acre. The house was cozy and roomy, with six bedrooms and five fireplaces.

Catherine began her years at Marlborough with "very little confidence," said a friend. It was a relief when her sister Pippa joined her at Marlborough the next year.

As the years passed, Catherine regained her confidence and began participating in school activities again. She played tennis, netball, and hockey on school teams, and was well-liked by the other students. A fellow student described her as "ordinary, hard-working, athletic, and easy-going."

Catherine finished her Marlborough years with three A-levels. A-levels are "advanced level" courses and exams that high school students in Britain study. Catherine earned A's in her math and art A-levels, and a B in English.

Meanwhile, Prince William was growing up an hour away. He was studying at Eton College, a boarding school for boys that many royal family members have attended. William graduated in the top 10% of his class with A-levels in geography, biology, and art history.

William's life was not carefree, because he always knew that one day he would become King of England. His grandmother was the current Queen, Queen Elizabeth. Since William was five, the Queen had invited him to have tea with her privately each week. During these times, she taught William about British history and about some of the things he should know when he became King.

William was grateful for these special times with his grandmother, especially because he didn't have a mother anymore. His mother, known as Princess Diana, had been killed in a car crash in Paris when William was just 15. Although his father, Prince Charles, did all that he could for William and his brother, Harry, William still missed his mother's love and support.

William and Catherine were each facing a big decision now: where should they attend college?

St Salvator's Quad, where William and Kate lived at St Andrews

Chapter 4

Meeting at the University of St Andrews

Catherine ran her hands through her wavy brown hair. She needed to decide where she would attend university. Neither of her parents had gone to college, and they were unsure of how to help her. Catherine had always been interested in art, and since the University of Edinburgh in Scotland had a great art program, she considered going there.

But Carole Middleton reminded Catherine that Prince William had decided to go to the University of St Andrews, also in Scotland. She felt that Catherine might enjoy going to college with the future King of England. How exciting that would be! Catherine had always felt a connection to Prince William. At Marlborough, she told friends that there were no boys at the school who she was interested in. "I don't like any of them, " she said. "There's no one quite like William. I bet he's really kind. You can just tell by looking at him."

Mrs. Middleton wasn't the only mother encouraging her daughter to attend school with Prince William. Applications to St Andrews were up 44% the year the prince started there, and 90% of those extra applicants were female.

William had decided on St Andrews because he loved Scotland. It was a hilly country, more open and less crowded than England. He was breaking royal tradition by going there, since most of his royal relatives had attended Oxford of Cambridge Universities. But William liked to make his own decisions. Besides, his housemaster at Eton had gone to St Andrews and had loved it. William decided to head to St Andrews to study art – just like Catherine.

In Europe, it is common for students to complete a "gap year" between their high school and college studies. During this year, some students work at a job. Others travel. Catherine spent time during her gap year studying art in Italy with a group of friends. She also spent time in Chile.

Prince William used his gap year to take part in military training in the Central American nation of Belize. Like Catherine, he also spent time in Chile, where he worked with children.

In the autumn of 2001, Catherine headed with her parents to St Andrews. She felt nervous as she stared out the car window at the foggy, quiet college town. Would she be happy here, or would she face hard times as she had at Downe House? Would she have a chance to see Prince William, or maybe even become friends with him? Kate crossed her fingers, smiled, and determined to do her best here.

Later, she joined a crowd of 3,000 who had gathered to see Prince William arrive at the university. Catherine stood in the back of the crowd, thinking how different William's arrival was from her own. Nobody had watched as she and her parents carried clothes and books to her dorm room.

As she stood on tiptoes to catch a glimpse of William, she noted sadness in his eyes. "I think he just wants to be left alone to have a normal college life," she told a friend. "But I suppose that's impossible." Catherine determined not to bother the prince – but soon their paths would cross.

Catherine soon learned that she and William lived in the same dorm, called St Salvator's. They were on different floors, but each had a similar small room, just 15 square feet – quite different from what William was used to in his royal homes. William had a bodyguard who lived in the dorm room next to his.

The prince woke up early so he could go jogging before most other students were awake. He liked his privacy, but he wanted to make friends as well. So during one of his first weeks at school, he invited a few other students to his room one evening to visit. One of the girls he invited was Catherine. She later recalled this first meeting: "I turned bright red, feeling very shy about meeting him," she said, not knowing that she and William would have quite a history together.

The village of St Andrews

Chapter 5

St Andrews Days

Knowing that Catherine liked Prince William, her friends began calling her "princess in waiting." But this princess would have a very long time to wait.

William and Catherine continued their friendship at St Andrews, but there was no romance at first. William dated other girls, and many of them didn't like all the attention and demands that came with a connection to a future king. One of his girlfriends broke up with him, saying, "I can't live like this!" She wanted to keep her privacy.

Neither William nor Catherine was totally happy during that first semester of college. Catherine considered switching to another school, and William did as well. But Catherine was always patient and realistic, and she decided to stick things out and stay. She convinced William to do the same. She suggested that he change his major from art history to geography. He did that, and was happier with his new field of study.

"Catherine is a very level-headed girl. She doesn't try and tell me what she thinks I should do. I like that," said William. "I am so tired of people telling me what they think I should do."

That winter, Catherine modeled in a fashion show at St Andrews to raise money for a charity. William paid over $300 for a front-row seat, and he saw Catherine in a whole new way. She wasn't the girl in casual jeans and sweaters that he was used to anymore. She looked tall (5'10"), pretty, and confident as she strolled the walkway. William knew she was dating a member of the school cricket team, but he was determined to get to know her better.

Catherine's boyfriend graduated that spring, and William quickly asked if Catherine would like to live in an apartment (which the British call a "flat") with him and two other students during the next school year. Feeling a bit awkward sharing an apartment with the future King, Catherine asked her mother's opinion. Mrs. Middleton told her that she felt it was fine, and so Catherine agreed.

Living in the same apartment, the prince and Catherine got to know each other better. William invited Catherine to the royal Scottish estate at Balmoral Castle. William's mother, Princess Diana, had always disliked the lonely, remote Scottish highlands, but Catherine loved it there. William introduced her to his father, Prince Charles. When Catherine turned 21 that year, William visited her home to meet her parents.

The university did all it could to protect Prince William's privacy. The news media also left the prince alone more than might be expected. Many felt that news photographers had been at least partly responsible for causing the car wreck that killed his mother, and so they felt that William should be given more privacy. This let William and Catherine begin their relationship without too many news photos or interviews.

During their two remaining college years, William and Catherine lived in a cottage with a large yard (or, as the British say, "garden") and six-foot walls around the edges to further protect their privacy. St Andrews students knew that the prince and Kate, as she was sometimes now called, were a couple. "Kate felt something for William straightaway," said a friend. "And he was all in for her, completely."

There were bumps along the way. As the future King, William was popular with the girls. Many of them wanted to date him. William enjoyed having a good time and spent time with some of these girls. Kate saw this and it made her doubt that she and William would have a future together.

As their university days came to an end, Kate and William each seemed to feel unsure about their relationship. They sat at graduation in their black robes, listening to the vice chancellor speak: "You will have made lifelong friends," he said. Then he smiled and looked in William and Kate's direction. "You may have met your husband or wife."

Watching the graduates from the audience were the members of the Middleton family – and also the Queen and her husband Prince Philip, and Prince Charles, and his wife Camilla.

When news reporters asked if he would marry soon, William

sounded annoyed. "I'm only 22. I'm too young to marry at my age. I don't want to get married until I'm at least 28 or 30."

Kate heard William's words on TV. Should she wait on her prince? Friends had said that Kate "was always the one you could trust to do the absolutely right thing." What was the right thing for Kate to do now?

Prince Harry and Catherine Middleton attend a ceremony

Chapter 6

Waity Katie

Now that college was over, William got busy with royal duties. He often visited charities and attended official events. For Kate, the future was less clear. Should she get a job? If she did, she would not be available to travel with William or to attend events with him. It was a confusing time for her.

Wanting to do something, Kate began her own business designing and selling children's clothing online. She felt that she would enjoy this and thought that the business would be successful. She also began working with a consultant who could help her dress in a more professional way so that she would look good when she traveled with William.

Meanwhile, William was following his dream of serving in the military. He began training to be a British Army officer at The Royal Military Academy Sandhurst. His brother, Prince Harry, was already at the training school. The training at Sandhurst was intense, and William was not able to see Kate very often.

Kate's clothing line for children struggled. She decided to take an office job with a British clothing store called Jigsaw. The store allowed Kate to work just four days each week, so that she would have plenty of free time for events with William. Kate continued to try to become more princess-like, dressing up in a style that seemed appropriate for a future royal family member.

When William graduated from Sandhurst, Kate stood out in the audience. She had chosen a bright red coat so that William and his family members, including the Queen, would be sure to notice her.

The news media had definitely noticed William and Kate as a couple, too. One store even began making William & Kate T-shirts, mugs, and plates, hoping for a royal wedding in the near future.

In January of 2007, Kate turned 25. Reporters began calling her "Waity Katie" because she and William had been dating for so many years. Now, the media was sure that Prince William would propose to Kate on her birthday. Camera crews waited outside the Middleton home, hoping that Kate would come out to make an announcement.

But behind the scenes, things were not so cheery. William had begun having second thoughts about his relationship with Kate. He told his father that he was feeling too much pressure from the press. William also was well aware that his own parents' marriage had been unhappy. Prince Charles was 32 and Diana had just turned 20 when they married. They had not known each other more than a few months. Despite a lovely start to their romance, Charles and Diana quickly realized that they had very different interests. Diana loved the excitement of London, while Charles preferred hunting and gardening in the country. He began seeing an earlier girlfriend named Camilla Parker Bowles again (now, after Diana's death, he had married her). Diana felt hurt at this and began finding male friends of her own. William didn't want to make the same mistakes his parents had.

Although Prince Charles had always liked Kate, he told his son to take his time and not to marry until he felt it was right. William was spotted at several nightclubs in London, where he was dancing and having a good time – with Kate nowhere in sight.

All of this hurt Kate's feelings, and again, she was confused over what she should do. She couldn't put her life on hold forever, waiting for William. She decided to move ahead, joining a rowing team where she met new friends and improved her strength.

After spending several months apart, William realized how much he missed Kate. He remembered the advice that his mother had given him: "If you find someone you love in life, you must hang onto that love and look after it. You must protect it." William decided that Kate was the one he wanted to spend his life with. They would not break up again.

In July, William and Harry attended a concert honoring their mother ten years after her death. The princes had worked hard to plan a concert their mother would have enjoyed. Kate attended as well, although she did not sit with William. But after the concert, the two celebrated together at a party.

Later that summer, William and Kate took a vacation to an island in the Indian Ocean. There, William reassured Kate by telling her that he planned to marry her. But, he also told her that he was not yet ready. Would Kate wait for him?

"Waity Katie" said yes.

Prince Charles' wife Camilla and Catherine

Chapter 7

Princess in Waiting

The next few years saw Kate preparing for her future role as William's wife. Royal officials had seen how hard it had been for William's mother, Princess Diana, to adjust to life in the royal family. They wanted things to be easier for Kate. So, she entered into royal activities little by little. Only William and Kate knew that they planned to marry, so Kate's future as William's wife had to be kept secret.

William invited her to the royal Scottish Balmoral Estate to go hunting – a popular activity with the royals. The couple often spent weekends together at Clarence House, Prince Charles's official London home. There, they enjoyed just relaxing and even cooking. William made mashed potatoes, with Kate grilling sausages.

Kate even stood in for William at some events, since he was now busy in the royal navy. She attended his cousin's wedding in his place, which showed the world that the royal family accepted her as one of its own. When a friend told Kate how lucky she was to be dating Prince William, Kate smiled. "He's lucky to be going out with *me!*"

How else did Kate fill her days? She knew that royals were heavily involved with charities, and so she selected a charity to support: the Starlight Foundation, which grants wishes to sick children. Even the four-day work weeks at Jigsaw had proven to be too difficult to fit in with her other activities, and so Kate quit that job and began to work full-time for her family's Party Pieces business. She updated the company's website and prepared their catalogs.

She waited and waited, doing whatever she could to keep William happy. She attended his polo matches to watch him play and went on trips with him when he had time off. One of the prince's friends said, "Kate is beautiful, sweet, and she likes to have fun. She's also very calm and cool, which William needs."

William and Kate attended many weddings together. Always, their friends would ask, "When will you two be getting married?" They got tired of the question. Kate had to wonder when William would finally feel ready. She had been ready for a long time!

Around this time, William decided on his next adventure. It was not marriage. Rather, he wanted to become a search-and-rescue pilot for the Royal Air Force. In this job, he would fly a helicopter on lifesaving missions to rescue people who had been swept out to sea or who were stranded in other ways. Once, William went out to rescue a mountain climber who had broken her leg. Imagine her surprise when she was rescued by the future King of England! The woman recovered, and later said, "It was a shock to find out (William) was flying the helicopter!"

Kate and Prince William ride in a carriage after their wedding

Chapter 8

Engagement

As 2010 came to an end, William invited Kate to join him on a trip to Kenya, Africa. William had traveled to Kenya several times and loved Africa, calling it "my second home." He usually stayed at the game preserve of his friends, the Craig family. The news media had reported that William and the Ian Craig's daughter, Jecca, were dating, but those days were long past. Now, William planned a trip with Kate that they both would always remember.

Before leaving for Africa, William asked his brother Harry for something very special. When their mother died, William and Harry had each gotten some of her items. William had chosen her watch, while Harry had asked for Diana's engagement ring. The beautiful ring featured a large blue sapphire surrounded by diamonds. Now, William asked if he could have the ring to give to Kate when he asked her to marry him. "It means a great deal to me, and I don't think Harry is getting married any time soon," William said. Harry loved Kate and was happy to hand over the ring.

William packed the ring gently in bubble wrap and slid it into his backpack. He checked it each day to be sure he didn't lose it. "I knew if it disappeared I would be in a lot of trouble!"

Kate and her prince spent their days enjoying the African wildlife and the beautiful views. They camped in tents some nights and relaxed in expensive lodges during others. On October 20, William suggested that they go fishing in a lake on the slopes of Mount Kenya. Kate was shocked when William put down his fishing pole and asked her to marry him!

Kate burst into tears. Even though William had told her they would get married someday, she had waited for so many years that it almost seemed impossible that she would really marry her prince. Finally, the dream had come true! "It was very romantic and very personal," she said of William's proposal, and William grinned as he added, "I was really pleased she said yes!"

Kate loved her ring. William said that using Diana's ring was "my way of making sure my mother didn't miss out on today."

Giddy with excitement, the couple wrapped up their trip and returned to London. They let their families know about the engagement, but otherwise kept the big news private until it could be announced officially.

That came on November 16, 2010, when Clarence House

announced William and Kate would marry the following spring or summer. After several times when the press wrongly thought that an engagement was coming, this time they were taken by surprise. The Queen was "absolutely delighted," and Prince Charles no doubt echoed Kate's thoughts by saying, "It has taken them a very long time."

Prince Harry shared his happiness as well: "It means I get a sister which I have always wanted."

William and Kate appeared at St. James Palace for the announcement. William wore a dark suit and Kate chose a royal blue dress to match her sapphire ring. They laughed and smiled like the friends they had been for nearly a decade.

The British people – as well as people all over the world – were happy with the news and wanted to know all about the couple. In a British TV interview, Kate explained how William "supported me through good times and also through bad times." William told viewers that his bride-to-be had "many habits that make me laugh and that I tease her about." He also shared, "When I first met Kate, I knew there was something very special about her."

This interview was the first time most of the public had ever heard Kate's voice. They liked what she said. When asked about her future in the royal family, she said, "I'm willing to learn quickly and work hard."

People already began wondering when William and Kate would have children. "Obviously we want a family so we'll have to start thinking about that," William said.

The whole nation seemed to breathe a sigh of relief. After so many years, Prince William had decided on a bride. Royal weddings were exciting for the whole country, and they gave people something to look forward to. The next several months would be full of planning and anticipation.

Westminster Abbey, site of William and Kate's wedding

Chapter 9

A Royal Wedding

For Kate, the days between her engagement and her wedding flew by quickly. She and William had many decisions to make.

First, they decided to hold their wedding at Westminster Abbey. The abbey, in downtown London not far from Buckingham Palace, is known as "the Royal church." All British coronations for the past thousand years have been held there, as well as many royal weddings. You'll find many of England's kings and queens buried there as well.

To bring a feel of outdoors into the huge abbey, William and Kate had trees brought in to line the aisle. And while many of the 2,000 wedding guests needed to be rulers of nations and other royals, William and Kate made sure that their friends made up a large part of the audience.

One decision was Kate's alone: her choice of dress. She began meeting with dress designers, although her dress was a closely-guarded secret right up to the moment she appeared in it on her wedding day.

April 29, 2011, dawned bright and sunny. One million Britons lined the London streets, hoping to catch a glimpse of the royal couple either before or after the wedding. On television, two billion more were glued to the action.

Excitement built as Prince William and his best man, Harry, arrived at the abbey. William surprised guests by wearing a red coat for his 11:00 morning wedding. Minutes later, a car pulled up with Kate inside. She had decided to travel by car rather than the more traditional carriage used by earlier brides. Her maid of honor, sister Pippa, waited to help arrange her dress.

The eyes of the world were on Kate as she emerged from the car. Her dress was beautiful, and simpler than Princess Diana's had been 30 years earlier – Diana's train of 25 feet was much longer than Kate's six-foot one. Kate's dress featured lace sleeves, and rose and shamrock designs she had selected. Her veil was secured with a tiara borrowed from the Queen.

"I think if William didn't have a public role, they would have loved to have gotten married in a little church in Bucklebury," one of their friends said. "It felt a bit like that – like a really personal event but on a larger scale."

After the ceremony ended, William and Kate headed back to

Buckingham Palace in an open carriage. Crowds cheered and waved British flags at the couple. "I'm so happy," Kate was seen to say to William. And why shouldn't she be? Although it had taken nearly ten years, she was finally married to her prince. Despite her youthful appearance, Kate at age 29 was the oldest woman to ever marry a future King of England.

The couple thrilled audiences outside the palace with an appearance on the balcony, where they kissed twice. They enjoyed two receptions at the palace, feasting on a fancy wedding cake adorned with the initials W and C and iced flowers. Finally, they drove off in Prince Charles' convertible, decorated with balloons and a license plate reading JU5T WED.

William and Kate tour Canada

Chapter 10

Royal Life

Two weeks after the wedding, Kate and William left on a ten-day honeymoon on a private island. Officially, they were now the Duke and Duchess of Cambridge: the Queen had given them these titles hours before their wedding. Someday, when Prince Charles becomes King, they will then become the Prince and Princess of Wales – although Kate will never officially be "Princess

Catherine" or "Princess Kate."

Although she had loved the excitement of planning her wedding, Kate was basically a private person. She was happy to settle down to a more normal life with William, in a small house on the island of Anglesey off the coast of Wales. William continued his work as a search-and-rescue pilot, and Kate enjoyed shopping at the local grocery store and cooking dinners.

Britain loved its new royal couple. They were young, attractive, and in love. The Queen asked them to attend many events, and they were busy right away with tours and official appearances. They went on a tour of North America during the first summer they were married, and the Canadians and Americans seemed to love them as much as the British did.

London hosted the summer Olympics in 2012, and William and Kate were spotted at many of the events – usually cheering British athletes. They adopted a Cocker Spaniel puppy they named Lupo.

2012 was a busy year for William and Kate, as well as the entire royal family. The Queen celebrated her Diamond Jubilee, marking 60 years she had served as Queen. During a week of summer events, William and Kate joined the other royals to honor the Queen.

Everywhere she went, the press was excited to report on Kate's clothes and every word she said. But there was something else that they were waiting and hoping for.

Kate and William leave the hospital with baby Prince George

Chapter 11

A Royal Baby

Most newly-married couples hope to have a baby. But it's especially important for royal couples. That's because Prince William and Kate's first baby will be the King or Queen of England someday. In the past, a boy would automatically become King someday. But if their first baby were a girl, she would only become Queen if she had no brothers.

This rule seemed old-fashioned, and politicians in Britain decided it was time to change it. After all, Queen Elizabeth had been Queen successfully for sixty years. Why not make sure that William and Kate's first child could lead England, no matter whether it was a boy or a girl? Parliament began work to change the rules, and just in time: in December 2012, the news reported that Kate was in the hospital. She was expecting a baby and was feeling quite sick.

After a few days, she was feeling better and was released. The media continued to report every detail about the coming baby: had Kate "slipped" and hinted that the baby was a girl? If so, would she be named "Diana" to honor William's mother? What types of clothes would Kate wear?

Soon, July arrived. It was the month of the baby's birth, and beginning July 1, cameras and reporters camped outside St Mary's Hospital in London, the same hospital where Prince William had been born 31 years earlier. "You have to get in there early. It's one of the biggest stories in the world right now," explained one photographer.

The Royal Mint, which makes British coins, announced that it would give lucky silver pennies to all British babies born the same day as William and Kate's baby.

Watchers all over the world tweeted #GreatKateWait as the July days passed with no baby. Kate had waited for her prince. She was now waiting for her baby, too.

Then, at 6:00 a.m. on Monday, July 22, William and Kate arrived at the hospital. The world waited for the royal baby to arrive.

At 4:24 that afternoon, a baby boy was born to the couple. He weighed 8 pounds, 6 ounces. He was third in line to the British throne, after his grandfather, Prince Charles and his father, Prince William.

The world rejoiced at the news. In London, the fountains at Trafalgar Square were colored blue in honor of the new baby. Niagara Falls were even lit up in blue! At Buckingham Palace, the royal band played a song called "Congratulations" at the changing of the guard ceremony. Shots were fired across the city to mark the birth, and bells at Westminster Abbey, where William and Kate got married, pealed for three hours.

The crowds did not leave St Mary's yet. They wanted to see William, Kate, and the new baby. The next day, they got their chance when the new family left the hospital. Kate and William dressed in blue, carrying the baby who was wrapped in a white blanket.

"He's got a good pair of lungs on him, that's for sure," said a proud Prince William. "He's a big boy, he's quite heavy" Then he looked at Kate, saying, "He's got her looks, thankfully."

"No, no, I'm not sure about that," Kate said, laughing. She added, "It's very emotional, it's such a special time. I think any parent will know what this feeling feels like."

William put the baby into a car seat, then into the car, and he drove the family away to Kensington Palace, where the Queen met her first great grandson. It was unusual for William, as a royal, to drive the car instead of having a driver. He said, "I think driving your son and your wife away from the hospital was really important to me. I don't like fuss, so it's much easier to do it yourself."

It is common for royal parents to wait a while before announcing a baby's name. Prince William's parents had waited a week to name him, and his father, Prince Charles, had not been named for a month! But just two days after William and Kate's baby was born, his name was announced. It was George Alexander Louis.

The name is a tribute to Queen Elizabeth's father, George VI, and grandfather, George V. As for the middle names, Prince Philip's grandfather was Prince Louis Alexander of Battenberg. Louis was also the name of Prince Philip's uncle Earl Mountbatten, a role model of Prince Charles. In the past 300 years, more English kings have been named George than any other name.

Someday, William and Kate's baby will reign as King George VII.

Kate (with Harry and William) wearing pink: is it a girl?

Chapter 12

A Little Princess

Life didn't slow down for William, Kate, and little Prince George. The public loved each photo that was released of the baby prince. Kate took many of those photographs herself.

When George was nine months old, his parents took him along on a tour of Australia and New Zealand. This trip echoed a similar journey that Prince William had taken with his own parents when he was a baby. George enjoyed visiting a zoo in Australia, where a bilby exhibit was named after him (a bilby looks like a desert rabbit). He even had a playdate with other toddlers while in New Zealand. Perhaps it's not surprising, since he will one day be king, that George helped himself to many of the toys in the room – even those that other children were playing with!

The family celebrated George's first birthday on July 22 with a party at Kensington Palace. Carole Middleton, Kate's mom, planned the party with a Peter Rabbit theme.

Just a few months later, exciting news was announced: Kate was expecting another baby! Kate again suffered from severe morning sickness. She cut back on her royal appearances, and enjoyed time with George. She told friends a funny story about the toddler. While Prince William was traveling, Kate told George that his dad was in China. George walked over to a china cabinet, looked inside, and said, "Daddy is not there."

The public began to wonder whether the new baby would be a girl. Kate and William did not find out before the baby was born. William's dad, Prince Charles, had always wanted a daughter. "We're hoping for a granddaughter!" he told a reporter.

Kate had said that her due date was mid to late April. Again this time, reporters and fans of the family camped out outside the hospital. And again, the days and weeks passed by without a royal baby.

Finally, early on the morning of May 2, William and Kate entered St Mary's Hospital by a side door. A few hours later, the news was announced: a little princess had been born! The public was thrilled when William, Kate, and the new baby appeared on the hospital steps later that same day. The baby was wearing a tiny yellow knit cap, and Kate was dressed to match, in a dress with yellow and white flowers. The family headed home to join Prince George.

Just as they had with George, William and Kate waited two days to tell the public the baby's name: Charlotte Elizabeth Diana. Charlotte is the female form of Charles, William's father. Elizabeth honors William's grandmother, Queen Elizabeth, and it is also Kate's middle name. Diana, of course, is a tribute to William's mother, Princess Diana. Many noticed that, as Kate left the hospital with little Charlotte, her engagement ring flashed over the top of the baby's blanket. The ring had first belonged to Diana, and it was as if she was saying that a bit of Diana could live on through this new little princess.

Chapter 13

Another Little Prince

William and Kate enjoyed their life with George and Charlotte. Since they are important members of the royal family, they had many official engagements. Still, they spent time together privately as a family whenever they could.

Kate wrote in a letter, "Spending quality time together is such an important aspect of family life and for me, as a mother, it is the simple family moments like playing outside together that I cherish." Speaking on a television show, William said, "Well, as the other parents in the room will testify, there's wonderful highs and there's wonderful lows. It's been quite a change for me, personally. I'm very lucky in the support I have from Catherine.

She is an amazing mother and a fantastic wife." Newspapers and magazine published photos of the family spending time together, playing outside.

The entire family went on a royal tour of Canada in autumn 2016, when Charlotte was just a year old and George was three. The children's nanny came along to watch them while William and Kate participated in formal events, but the public was most excited when the children made appearances too. At a party for military families, guests loved watching George ride a miniature horse and play with a bubble machine. Charlotte loved playing with a dog and a rabbit, and had a good time with balloon sculptures.

Life moved on, with George and Charlotte both starting preschool. William's brother Harry announced his engagement to American actress Meghan Markle.

Then, in September 2017, Kate had to cancel an engagement due to illness. This had happened before, and soon, Buckingham Palace announced the reason: she was expecting a third baby, in the spring!

Again, people wondered whether the baby would be a boy or a girl. Again, people waited outside the hospital as Kate's due date approached.

On the morning of April 23, 2018, Kate and William went to the hospital at 8:30. The wait was not long: at 11:01 a.m., a baby boy was born. The University of St Andrews offered congratulations to William and Kate, its former students. William came out of the hospital, and returned shortly with George and Charlotte. The gathered crowd loved watching Charlotte wave as they went in to visit Kate and the new baby.

Just before 6:00 that evening, William and Kate appeared on the hospital steps with their new baby. Kate and the baby were already going home. She wore a bright red dress. Some said it might be a tribute to William's mom, Princess Diana. Diana had worn a red coat when leaving the hospital with her second son, Prince Harry.

The public had to wait four days before the baby's name was announced on April 27: Louis Arthur Charles. The name Louis had a family connection, as many men in the royal family have Louis as part of their names (Prince William and Prince George both have Louis as a middle name). Although you might think the name is pronounced "Loo-is," the British say "Loo-ey." The name Arthur is a middle name of Prince William and also of his father, Prince Charles. And of course, Charles is the name of baby Louis' grandfather.

No doubt Kate will enjoy watching his personality emerge as he grows up. Will he be similar to his brother George? Will he share traits with Princess Charlotte? Currently fifth in line to the throne, Louis is unlikely to ever become king.

Queen Elizabeth II and her husband, Philip, at her 1953 coronation

Chapter 14

The Future

One day, William and Kate will most likely become England's King and Queen. But that day may be many years away. William's grandmother, Queen Elizabeth, is in good health in her 90s and has already been Queen for over sixty years. Her mother lived to be 101. After the Queen dies, William's father, Prince Charles, will become King. He has waited his whole life in preparation to be King.

When the time comes, Kate will become the sixth Queen Catherine. Three of the previous Queen Catherines were married to the famous King Henry VIII! William will be the fifth King William.

Until that time, Kate will no doubt keep busy with her children and her charities, which focus on children, art, and people overcoming addiction.

From ordinary baby to bullied child to future queen, Kate Middleton – now Duchess Catherine – has come a very long way. "One of Catherine's best assets is that she has always been very sure of herself," said a friend. "She has never allowed herself to be influenced by others." That quality will serve her well as she continues to be one of the most famous women in the world.

Timeline of Kate Middleton's Life

1982: Kate is born

1987: Mike and Carole Middleton begin Party Pieces business

1992: Kate first sees Prince William when he visits her school to play in a hockey match

1995: Kate enrolls at Marlborough College

2000: Kate spends her "gap year" in Italy

2001: Kate and Prince William meet at the University of St Andrews

2002: William and Kate become housemates

2006: Kate and William graduate from St Andrews

2007: William and Kate split up and get back together again

2010: The Palace announced the engagement of Prince William and Kate

2011: William and Kate are married and become the Duke and Duchess of Cambridge

2013: Prince George Alexander Louis is born to William and Kate

2015: Princess Charlotte Elizabeth Diana is born to William and Kate

Timeline of the World

1982: Prince William is born

1987: Margaret Thatcher becomes England's longest-serving Prime Minister since the early 19th century

1989: Berlin Wall falls

1995: OJ Simpson is found innocent of the murder of his ex-wife, Nicole Simpson

1996: Prince William's parents, Charles and Diana, divorce

1997: Prince William's mother, Diana, is killed in a car crash in Paris

2000: Queen Elizabeth, the Queen Mother, turns 100

2001: Terrorist attacks on the World Trade Center in the US

2002: Europe begins using the euro as currency

2004: George W. Bush is re-elected President of the US

2005: Prince Charles marries Camilla Parker Bowles

2012: Queen Elizabeth II celebrates 60 years on the throne

2016: Donald Trump is elected US President

ABOUT THE AUTHOR

Susan Barnett Braun has been fascinated by the British royal family since Diana, Princess of Wales, came onto the scene in the early 1980s. Susan wrote her high school senior research paper on "Charles and Diana: The Royal Romance." Her teacher did not approve of the topic at first, but he changed his mind after reading the paper.

Susan taught elementary school for eight years. She has traveled to England to study on a Lilly Teacher Creativity Fellowship, and has researched the wives of King Henry VIII through a National Endowment for the Humanities grant. She enjoys staying current on royal news.

She heartily thanks Caroline Braun, Isabel Braun, and Sophie Braun for help with the book cover and publicity. Gratitude as well goes to Lisa Hayes and Elaine Schulte for editing.